# [ABOUT]NESS

THE HUGH MacLENNAN POETRY SERIES

Editors: Allan Hepburn and Carolyn Smart

Recent titles in the series

# [about]ness

**EIMEAR LAFFAN**

McGill-Queen's University Press
Montreal & Kingston • London • Chicago

ISBN 978-0-2280-1902-2 (paper)
ISBN 978-0-2280-1971-8 (ePDF)
ISBN 978-0-2280-1972-5 (ePUB)

Legal deposit third quarter 2023
Bibliothèque nationale du Québec

Printed in Canada on acid-free paper that is 100% ancient forest free
(100% post-consumer recycled), processed chlorine free

Funded by the Government of Canada    Financé par le gouvernement du Canada    |    Canada    Conseil des arts du Canada    Canada Council for the Arts

We acknowledge the support of the Canada Council for the Arts.

Nous remercions le Conseil des arts du Canada de son soutien.

---

**Library and Archives Canada Cataloguing in Publication**

Title: [About]ness / Eimear Laffan.

Names: Laffan, Eimear, author.

Series: Hugh MacLennan poetry series.

Description: Series statement: The Hugh MacLennan poetry
series | Poems.

Identifiers: Canadiana (print) 20230443370 | Canadiana (ebook)
20230443435 | ISBN 9780228019022 (softcover) |
ISBN 9780228019725 (ePUB) | ISBN 9780228019718 (ePDF)

Classification: LCC PS8623.A357765 A76 2023 |
DDC C811/.6—DC23

---

This book was typeset by Marquis Interscript in 9.5/13 Sabon.

Can I be so [      ] as to call this [       ]?

[       ]   *My Life*

"I went abroad once" / writes Zbigniew Herbert in
"A Life" / there was a time I entered the change room
of every sentence for the mirror / each reflection a new
costume / hung on the frame of my skeleton / an
occasional bone I threw myself / to quiet the subcutaneous
rattle // the antonym of "abroad" is "domestic," Google
suggests / what if my domestic is abroad / to say nothing
of its ancestral station at the stove / Herbert was off on
holiday to the Black Sea / my plan was fealty to the banks
of the Spree / the city-lord withdrew authority / I exiled
myself to the ministry of mountains and monotony / a
ghost to all my unlived lives // is there space to breathe /
in a text conceived under a hefty rubric / I cut at the
canopy for a little more light / what anyway is a life / I
have sat on an ashram floor calling to Ganesh to remove
all obstacles / "*om gam ganapataye namaha*" / I stayed
away from the temple when I bled / [insert your personal
mantra here] / I watch *Twin Peaks* three decades late / find
the male gaze unsettling / still I write aubades as Agent
Dale Cooper / how the past is a chess move that follows
you to the land of Douglas firs / the body host to a
wound that keeps returning / the environment overlaid
with sign // it was only after Ganesh lost his head that
he acquired a trunk with the replacement / perhaps the
boy needed a modicum of elephant to become / more
himself      more godly / every gift-curse narrative a
Valium cradle to rock self to sleep / nobody foregrounds
the headless mammal / for gods to live certain images
need to disappear

I passed the baton of my life from country to country[1] /
snippets of disparate languages torqued my mouth my
throat my tongue / Welsh I cannot spell    *contradizzione*
보고싶어요 / a biography of borrowed conveyances /
when I sang *zindagi ab tum hi ho* I addressed an asylum /
a facility of straitjackets tucked in low mattresses / this a
syntax born of contraception / the romance of that script
lost to my hand // "your mother and father met at a
dancehall" / says the voice that transits wire to nest in my
ear / naïve stranger who believes in love's durability / the
poems of my father keep / getting snagged on the death /
I need to be a novitiate / of the new order first // only
once did a Russian sailor stalk me / I had no desire to
encounter / the daze of faces on the street / "teacher
teacher teacher" / the trawler went on standing in the
dock / "go back home," the *Gallery* boys flapped their
cloths / in the night outside you could catch a crab with
an articulated claw / this an act we thought to do and we
did it / coin after coin into the slot / until we had a live
crustacean / no idea what to do with this life / we gave
it away to the unsleeping // somewhere a man in a trailer
handfeeds an endling greens / the small of a snail in the
soft shell of his palm / we act out of the theories given us,
says Wittgenstein / when Ungaretti wrote "Soldati" he
needed no more than autumn leaves / there is a limit to
this language game[2] / a soldier and a solitude in every
die cast


보고싶어요      I miss you
*zindagi ab tum hi ho*    you are my life

the tenant upstairs bounces a ball off the midnight walls /
minutes rent into a count / desire recedes the sculptor of
heads warrants / eyes sunk in sockets unlocked by her index
finger / no more am I twenty-five and high on hormones /
I bleed less and less / a million crystals build community in
my kidney / calcium     oxalate // doesn't [want] just change
form / move out from the body to set up shop elsewhere /
form sets thought free, says the classicist / am I to believe /
the problem of my life my existence the problem of my
anxiety is formal[3] // a field of grit rests beneath my prone
consciousness / the moon does not think to seduce me / is
a life redeemable I ask / why do I lack the proficiency / to
say I would not cash it in / exchange my receipt for another
torn piece of paper // over and over I wake to a pre-dawn
snow / over and over I make the mistakes I denigrate / cold
and if interior were assigned a colour / unequivocal blue

in
som
nia
is
a
lo[4]

ng
line
on
the
mar
gin[5]

"duckies duckies duckies," says the old man on the shoreline /
the small boy undying inside him / the photographer lauded
the idea of dying young / what he was after was the fame that
came post hoc / he was no Jeff Buckley     no Jesus     no
Timothy McVeigh // at university I studied castration anxiety
opportunity cost     structural strain theory / the sexual
exploitation of Tamil women used to recruit them to the
Tigers' female wing / "I have no country now but self," wrote
Jean Arasanayagam / "you are very quiet," my professor said
/ discussion had turned to the IRA / I did not want my
nationality to implicate me / "no nation now but the
imagination," Walcott put in Shabine's mouth / impossible to
control a reading tendency to boomerang every **persona** into
the author's body // on the east shore a conference of red-
headed turkey vultures rise into the air / a fresh constellation
of mosquito bites star my calf / a body can roam as a text can
roam / with limits / a text can roam as a body can roam /
sometimes / "you are such an Irish poet," a Caribbean writer
tells me / I recognise no names / on the list of names she
submits as **proof**

a singular god reigned on the island of my childhood / if I
had fulfilled the promise of indoctrination / this god (safe to
assume it's a "he") would be cast in capital / a difference
easier split than an inheritance // I took the executor to task /
chopped the Psalms until what remained was an Eros /
"blessed be he who delivers me in the garden my whole flesh
corruption"[6] / I ravaged the book for a name to replace
the name I could not name / or would not name / in this
small way I erased him / caused him to disappear into an
ameliorated order / Jakob Jakov Yakup Yakub / to supplant
to circumvent      to assail / a textual act no match for
████████████ / (yes) (I ██████████) (████████████████) /
(or) // the problem with gods is their sticky / no *liebe* of
Nietzsche severs sap from conscience / certain nights you are
called to your knees at the foot of the bed / you want to be a
good devotee      gracious      co-operative / was I jealous /
the whole world in seven days seven nights that whole lark /
I refuse to grant him exclusive rights to creation / I too am
searching for divine dispensation / call it transposition / mercy
summoned to the dark room / if only I was not squatting like
Canaan / on land that had names before the names we name
it / how easily I abdicate the singular pronoun / to what
address can I return the curse / of the capital father

certain poems have no qualms about being located /
they walk New York streets on their lunch hour / if I use
Steller's jay as placeholder / do you fathom the flight /
Trevor Benbulbin Llanbadarn Rajpur in no particular
order / that once we cohered is such a dream / Natalie
Diaz's salutary "good dreaming" conveys me to sleep
with care // certain nights I write snow / to situate myself
inside its "o" / I was never the kind of girl to lay down
in a snow pile / for the sake of an angel / should I die no
one will scour my drive / to salvage the rune / should
I send my body off a cliff as in a teenage vision / cruelty
the gift that keeps on reproducing // the engineer
modified the ship to anchor his worth / the wine bill
turned sour / is a debt payable if the timbers are rotten /
my personal madeleine a cheap cherry Chilean / the
assonance an accident of appetite // there was no
choreography on deck / only an [          ] conceived of
a wave / [                              ] / I am wasting the stores
to a fine tip / hands splintered from days exchanging
planks / ships adapt in the wake of theoretical captains /
Karl Marx has become a project manager according to
LinkedIn // I dreamt a field of scotch broom / yellow
jackets filling the air / as far as the ochre horizon / not
should I die / when and how / under the sway of which
interest / which scent

a draft of the preceding pages received the following comments:

this is projection and
not introjection

> (Added to the list of potential
> future work: *Odi et Amo, A
> Misplaced Diction of Therapy.*)

the reader cruises
the author. do you
like Barthes?

> (*A Lover's Discourse* needs
> reading at least twice: once
> when you are in love, once when
> you are adamantly not. I am
> allowing the awkward adverb to
> stand. *Why do I do that, you are
> perhaps asking?* This is John
> Godwin's 1999 translation of
> a line from Catullus's "Odi et
> Amo." Repetition occurs in
> a life, desired or otherwise.
> Consider Freud.[7] This whole
> project might be placed under
> the sign of "the desire to return
> to an earlier state of things."
> *This might be true, but it is not
> the whole story*, Lauren Berlant
> supposedly once cautioned a
> friend. It fits many a skeleton.)

this is very Joyce

> (*Ulysses*, scored for a dollar, sits
> unread on my shelf. Though
> I have taken instruction from
> Molly's yesses. The context was
> different. There was no Leopold
> on his knees at Howth Head.
> Afterwards we went for a pint
> by the DART. I have an interest
> in people on their knees. Actual.
> Figurative. Self. Other. Sex.
> Prayer.)

> ((I fucking wish. Prurient?))

this is a night-long
meditation

> (An insomnia that insists.)

there are some good lines
for your biographer here

> (Why did this feel like a threat?)

I see guilty men
everywhere

> (Clarified as pertaining to *their*
> life, but I can understand
> a window.)

turn left where the garage
used to be

> (This person understood me.)

I watch the coots mid-journey / as a colleague pings me /
to draft an SOP around loss / my life is my procedure / not
for all the Italians / consigned to the underworld with
Dante / does redemption keep / I do not want my head
turned / backwards in the next life // certain moments
I indulge / the illusion of a "next" / if I win the cash I'll
splurge on the OED / I am turned / every which way in
this lease // a friend who once had a visceral distaste for
wasps / now plants alyssum to attract the former enemy /
invites the small bundles / to address the little ant cow
pests / attached to her cannabis plants / what is my ploy /
do I summon paradise or the knowledge of a high //
"every I is a fiction finally," writes Walcott / breaking
the line after "a" / how to represent this cut / in a
preponderance of virgules / this free fall into a future /
[choose your own adventure] // I would like my life to
submit / to the tidy of iambic tercets / it stalls before the
silk screen of language / if there were a procedure for
living / I would adhere

I used to worship men / like Gods the best of them fail to
become / for I was taught to kneel / at the foot of affliction /
stopping at the station of every wound / & once the round
was done / impious not to begin again // there is a moment
in a poem's construction / when the longing is / to drag
the reckoning / toward some finite conclusion / some
accounting worth the salt / as if to wipe a forehead clean
of sweat / were also to remove the whiff / it does not
remove it / odour is more than a proposition // once a
stranger told me I was a lighthouse / "all light or dark and
no in between" / I absorbed the lightning bug intent / flew
far from this coastline / took my war to a cavern / lay my
body down in its dark / by the pulse of onyx wings / bats
know a fatal composition / they kept me from their
tongues / but one among the congregation / lay his grace
wing on the hill of my belly / I call this sincerity // if it were
not a sentimental metaphor / I would tell you the lighthouse
bulb is always on / the flashing an effect of a rotating
lens / oh I know I am a charlatan / wanting it every which
way / to tell you and not to tell you simultaneously / it is
only that I am / enamoured with refraction / desperate to
bend / what little light you perceive

in secondary school my geography teacher had one glass
eye / impossible to tell who she held in her gaze / if I was the
one called on / to answer the length of a lake / to delineate
the layers beneath crust // is self a noun stratified / by all
this sounding / I watched my mother lose the nounscape /
"daughter," I said / "daughter," she said / like a child
sampling a new word / in the black hole of her mouth / "your
dog is ugly," says my four-year-old friend / I have no dog to
satisfy his growing vocabulary / once I had a dog called
Zuppy / also a swing set    a father figure    a hedgerow
vision of a future // once when I was leaving my mother asked
me / what my mother thought of my departure / a measure
of lost relation inside her // I have a fantasy of a life / where
language runs to a tally that exceeds presence / allows love to
eke out / the sides of my every mouth / this no apology // the
shortest poem I ever wrote I called "No Apology" / its body
two words / "See title" / I understand silence / can be a litmus
test for character / consider Ovid / banished to Tomis by
Augustus / for an unknown error / something he wrote
perhaps / that did not impress the Emperor / some say his exile
was only ever a literary device / whether it was experience or
circuitry / its seaboard occupied his sea / without history we
would not be / here / your body next to my body / efforting to
constellate experience / if I erase my errancy I too disappear /
"did I go to bed last night," my mother asks me / we are so
very tired

let's imagine missives could arrive / at other than a void /
could find communion in the world / Dublin mornings I
eavesdropped on prison officers / coming off nightshift at
the Joy / batch after batch of toast I laid on tables / with the
prerequisite smile / how a pure feeling was the nominative
granted a prison I don't know / a thousand prayer flags do
not make for prayer // I read somewhere / our obligation as
sentients is to transform our desire / to make it something
other / this seemed to me to say / lay down your life / I was
unwilling to engage / such a surrender // there's a single
rower out there on the lake / fluid of back and shoulder /
every stroke meeting the acquiescence of water / the turn to
pastoral an escape hatch / how does one bring another into
this world / forgetting what it takes to crawl / out from
under every epigraph // the officers ushered me passed
security / to the performance of a Martin McDonagh play /
all I can remember is a hand held to a hot stove / the thick
of uniforms three sides of the theatre / the holding / went
on / for an endless time // out from under every epigraph is
a nice idea / praxis is where the world runs out of steam /
I stumble[d] / out into the pre-set streets / I have always
been free to leave

my body was once a hotel lobby wall / clocking time
in three zones / mother    mountain    valentine of a
disjunctive heart / certain nights my scapula parted into
wings and the subjunctive slept / ah the lull of certain
nights / sheer curtains / under the draw of a warm wind //
my osteopath breaks my reverie / "place a cushion under
your soul while lying on a flat surface" / sacrum subsumed
by predictive text / he endeavours to correct / "the vortex
of emptiness" / behind the cage of my ribs // I am failing
my life / unable to get out of the brake / only this and this
and this in my pack / thyme    dirt    rift // once I made
a den of tarpaulin and silence / I'd flip the blue door of
retreat open / lay down in the moss of childhood inquiry /
only the river and I cognizant of time's seam / or so I
thought // I have been wanting / [nothing new in this] / to
see everything at once / to acquire the compound eyes of
a dragonfly / when what is needed is a box of plasters / to
draw the split ends of self closer together / to nurture an
alternate memorandum of understanding / as in a grid by
Agnes Martin / "On a clear day #1 1973" say // the alarm
bells clang / #1 is one of many / one of a sequence of many
sequences / even on a clear day there are more variations
than one can lever / any attempt to pin time calls up clouds
/ stratus    funnel    obdurate / an assertion of atmosphere /
out of our control / a snow storm    a heat dome / a dusk
of red cadmium / this blur under these smoke-strained skies

an interlude on the order of relationality [culled from
unborn embryos]:

in the beginning the mouth
I inside it
a thumb sucked on

for a decade I set
my bent on I's erasure
dependence embarrassed me
every parasite in need of a host

all night we went pandal to pandal
returning to watch the sun rise
over the broken Kolkata suburb
there was an us to speak of
a sliver of liver

his we was obligated elsewhere
a teenage cut
no grand epiphany
a reveal bash on repeat

the audacity of speaking
a we I was
low to behold

my nan used to coax needle after needle / through white
cloth / to make a petal or a sepal / shallow rivers hemming
her hands / their blue exhuming from some recess of my
hippocampus / a canopy of cobalt / I watch my brothers
haul / over a cut grass mountain / polyethylene tight
against the evening / stones at the foot of the tarp / to
keep it from blowing away // the ancients used to sew
stories / into the hem of the hero's cloak / the moral to
live / close to the skin / a silo to be drawn from / when
circumstance caused breath to thin // this side of the
ocean / fireweed blankets the forest floor / in the wake
of devastation / blooms awoken from a nascent state / a
purple proxy for the spent forest / as the eager scavenge /
what makes for honey


needle after needle

stories in

to proxy

the barista calls out "Eve" / for a moment I forget / this
paper cup is my destiny / if a matrix of this work exists /
it alights in the furrows / an accident of production / this
geography cannot pronounce me / if I finish this manuscript
in its holding cell / I'll grant myself permission to leave /
a receding tide can ground a vessel / the sailors tell me //
I grew up next to a river / knelt with my grandmother /
at the foot of her brass bed / in absentia she frowns at my
demotion of the sky god / to the rank of myth / I reinvest
what belief I can muster into the body / in Christian
theology this makes me / both [          ] and [          ] //
"I miss not having had a Catholic initiation," says Tara /
saved years of recovery / born inside a surveillance state /
breaking up with God is no easy feat / could all the angels
please depart the living room of my frontal lobe // the
carpenter of my anecdote / wanted the continuity of his
genes / I liked the rough of his hands / the goodbye letter
carved of cherry wood // when Stevens lost God he found
poetry / a critic says Williams would not have arrived / at
the great poems / without first the elasticity / *Kora in Hell*
had to precede broken green bottles in hospital courtyards /
I am scouting for excuses for verbosity / have a good
dustbin handy, says Szymborska / sound advice even as
I pour its potential contents / into a too vast silo // perhaps
this poem is a pallbearer / who does not know it's time to
retire / the box heavy yet familiar / at least a pallbearer
knows / the industry it operates within / the terminal draft /
where else but hell would Kora have gone

in Varanasi I sent wishes down the river / in the form of
marigolds and squat tea-light lamps / the miniature fires
of my desires / burning out fast in the water / without the
good grace / to do so out of my purview / "purview" is a
word I have been told not to use / "what is the function
of this diction"[8] / my traps so tender / my shoulders
hunch to the screen // in Dehradun I could count on the
numerologist / to always be sat under the same tree / a
reading for fifty one rupees / one hundred and one if your
question was a conundrum // the translation I was given /
was short of the words spoken / an edit that may have
been a kindness / an act of reparative justice in advance of
the deathblow / I placed a hundred in the reader's hand /
was it inauspicious to borrow the shagun / I was reading
Tanizaki at the time / naïve of shadow time

> Supplementary reading:
> *In Praise of Shadows* by Jun'ichirō Tanizaki
>
> which I open at random
>
> "... but do we prefer a pensive luster to a
> shallow brilliance ..." (11)
>
> "I know of nothing whiter than the face of
> a young girl in the wavering shadow of a
> lantern ..." (33)
>
> "When the rice is done, it should be cooled
> thoroughly ..." (40)

I did not ask Bishop's question: "Should we [I] have
  stayed at home?"

as a child I was dispatched to piano lessons / a stand-in
for another child's wish / "you are not trying," pronounced
the instructor / "I am giving it my heart and soul" / the
phrase jumped out of her mouth / a substitute for the absent
metronome / it is not difficult to see I plunder the past /
"don't tell anyone," my brothers said / each of their
mouths a small chimney / a sketch in smoke // once
I rounded the corner of our yard / on my red Raleigh
Apple / cracked the guitar slung across my back / both of
us cement-scratched / it was not always pronounced / the
panic in the small room of my chest / stethoscope displaced
as instrument / the beat in surround sound / a text does not
vanish an excess of ash / does not draw heavy metals from
soil // once I fell [please another verb] in love-lust with an
attic gardener / he blew weed into the night of my mouth /
counted aphids on the abacus of sleep / I can still taste / the
indent that ran / the long of his hip flexor / how do you
think / memory operates

<br>

                       crack

                                      the

                  verb

in      my mouth                             taste

               the                  soot

"I love God" / a poet says at her book launch / she laughs
a laugh of light / a laugh like the cotton of a gossypium / an
Ariel of air late spring / spirit is having a time / let me say it /
I miss God / I sought a house of forever / in clouds that
emptied into rain / I did not outlast my doubt // the bandura
player closes his eyes / he's listening for something / waiting
for the right silence to begin / his strings tuned to Shevchenko /
the Ukrainian exiled by Tsar Nicholas / condemned not to
write or paint / at the edge of empire / the artist does not
comply / "if it be rags, let it be rags" // outside two men go
on / about church     bodybuilding     the gym / about "saying
no like you mean it" / for Narcissus it would have all went
wrong / as soon as he hit the gym / no escape where every wall
is a lake // "vita est brevis; ars longa" / declares today's email
blast / you too could subscribe / to Latin Word of the Day /
divest from Facebook // which iterations of "no" are apt / to
be ignored in this reckoning / its utterance a pea under
so many mattresses / God in the ditch again / the night a
protracted dark / the weak heel advancing on the residuum //
in one version of her life / the battle is fought for Helen / in
another she is the excuse / "what is the mind of the Greeks
and you concerning my life" / Euripides has her ask
Menelaus / it is time for their return to Sparta / outside the
text the war never ends / when the war is over / the war begins

some [indictments] on the prior pages:

this is a slurring kind
of word

> (You will not find the word
> referred to here in this
> manuscript, though a trace
> element remains. It was a word
> I had recently fallen for and what
> self new to love is careful with an
> exuberance of feeling, does not
> attempt to sprinkle it where it
> does not belong? Who wants to
> know you are "in love"? Perhaps
> your mother.)

I'm questioning the form
of this stanza compared
to the rest of the poem

> (I had given the lines in question
> a single horizon. Not for the
> favoured a crowded field,
> an overwhelm of offshoots. A
> moment when I thought, oh yes,
> *these lines*. What arrogance such
> a writer possesses. Who was I to
> tell a reader what they should
> attend to. These lines have been
> incorporated into the broader
> form and it is to my satisfaction
> you will never know which lines
> they are. I'm quite sure you'll
> cope. Are you even here?
> Loitering in an almost margin.)

((The distance from margin
to marginalia is an "i" and
an indefinite article. How is an
indefinite eye to corral its gaze?))

this might be a kill your
darlings occasion

(I did not want to kill it. Instinct
said preserve the mess of
bearing, the unbiblical carnage.
This is my excuse for everything.
And as someone in your life
should have informed you,
an excuse is no sister to the
apology. A sister-wife maybe.)

((What constitutes a true
apology? Categorically not a
$10 tillandsia sent by air-mail
in the absence of a terrarium to
house it – an air plant cannot
live on air alone. I was charmed
by the visible trichomes. The
moment passed. An apology
needs a measure – the mien the
message.))

((("Categorically?" Why do I let
adverbs my acreage to perform
their waggle dance? Stet. It's a
distance from here to the hive.)))

this morning is a dove / sent ashore to take stock of the
plot / it changes you / waking in a hull alone / everybody
knows the animals go / two by two into the future / I did
not read this as salvation / the stranded left behind to
watch the water rise / a tease between their toes / ankles
mired in mud // say you gave up God / the current at your
calves / black sand at the shore of you / say you woke
each day / paper fish on your back / your sluice box
dammed with pyrite / each tributary refusing to give up
the gold / this is how to become / a ghost in a ghost
town / a miner in the wrong century / language-drunk
on filings // say the conditional is not a game you play for
fun / you are nailed tight to its cross / a wreath in lieu of
a pew // once a "friend" told me I was destined for hell /
I was always meeting myself in the world / better this
than to live as an amnesiac / no sense of the loss you were
conceived of / the dove intones its method / a laud in
my dawn ear / coo      coo      coo

once & once & once

███████████████
███████████████
███████████████
█████████ / I am not
doing a good job of all this
selfing // ████████████
███████████████
███████████████

█████ / there are two kinds of
people / ██████████████

*"'She' is indefinitely
other in herself. That
is undoubtedly the
reason she is called
temperamental,
incomprehensible,
perturbed, capricious –
not to mention her
language in which
'she' goes off in all
directions …"*
– *Luce Irigaray*

// it can be unclear which camp a
person falls inside / they give
mixed messages / kisses and
dunches / lunches with logos /
mouths contract-full of tender

[                    ] an act of de-lapidation

here I stand with what little ceremony / under the
panopticon of all the fathers / I spread my Rider-Waite
out / on the black glass Italian table / worry an excess
of modifiers / can upset a terroir / there is so much life one
can enumerate / always there'll be more // Eliot did not
want his capital-L life to be written / even thought to will
it / your job will be "to supress everything suppressible" /
he told his executor / I do not will / all I do not possess /
T.S's pillow of dirt / as are those of all the fathers / at night
my head meets goose feathers / a temporary substitute //
I draw from the deck the six of swords / a raft between
two shores / when I talk of fathers / the problem is one
of tense / not every daughter seeks sanctity for her author /
father father father father / I pile the clay on further / after
God it gets easier / to bury the rest

fire number N71382, suspected cause lightning, approximate location Harrop Creek, estimated size 2,126 hectares, fire of note

fire number N51610, approximate location Ladybird 1, estimated size 0.01 hectares, stage of control new

fire Number N51611, Ladybird 2, Ladybird 1's twin, 0.01 hectares, stage of control new

fire number N61612, suspected cause person, approximate location Gilpin Grasslands, estimated size 0.01 hectares, stage of control new

fire number N51470, lightning, Battle Mountain, 75 hectares, active, modified response

fire number V10484, suspected cause person, Harrison Lake East, 202 hectares, fire of note

K20637, person, Elephant hill, 110,236 hectares, fire of note

N41369, lightning, 3.4km west of Sorcerer Mountain, 300 ha, modified response

C31489, person, Lynx creek, 100, active

I look down the long of water / someone thought to
dam / knowing a dam alters an ecosystem / & so it goes //
each year Kokanee colour the channel / a pilgrimage
constituted / by biology and return / cells with their way
of knowing origin / not that I have purchase on this
romanticism / we may get to my bad blood with Keats //
once I pulled an oblong of colour / from the marsh by
Fisherman's / surely any part of nature that was yellow /
would light up a room / not for nothing is it's moniker
skunkweed / if **you live** in a landscape devoid of the
animal / you may not know the piss scent / the overcome
left in their wake // **empirically** the five stages of grief
have been disproven / I would like to have spent more
hours / watching the weather from a window seat / I was
busy / wielding my cutlass in a thicket of disbelief // the
salmon forge a path upstream / into the liquid arm of their
end / *quid tu facies* / in the meantime of another mean

in the pigeon occupied ruins of rail town / an upturned
trolley splays the air with castor wheels / smidgeons of
green emerge from rotten sleepers / "Paul loves Janie"
is chalked on the half-wall / does Janie love Paul back / if
you endeavour to live [love] life / does life reciprocate //
once I wrote a portrait of a lover as unclosed doors / his
pantry propped open by olive oil jars / three tiers of a
toolbox yawning / inside an open hallway closet / do I
wish this were metaphor[9] / doors close so fast / I am often
dizzy with the spin of stars / I dawdle after the event / like
a toddler after an apathetic parent // "from where I was
standing you seemed to be enjoying yourself" / words
I heard spoken / the speaker not mistaken / like Ester
Nilsson I was happy with my misguided contentions /
until I was not / the spur dawned a new day // "it's
apparent that [                    ]" / an observer appends
/ the stall of a face / subject to (mis)interpretation / "the
bias against quiet can cause deep psychic pain" / writes
Susan Cain in *Quiet* / yes Susan / yes


You can become acquainted
with Ester Nilsson in Lena
Andersson's *Wilful Disregard*.

as a child I was called / my fathers's daughter    my
brother's sister / was anxious to live in mouths / in
my own right / trusting a name granted residency / of a body
so avowed / making the mistake a naming amounts / to
a knowing // A was wont to call me Simran / "Simran"
from Sanskrit meaning an act of remembrance / or God's
gift / neither of which I cared to equate to / his intention
the transliteration prior to the translation / a nod to the
ruminant / he fancied me to become / he did not know
Eimear means "swift" / the hamster wheel and I intimates /
nights spent on the run[10] // I thought if I could learn
the names of things / I might feel (more) (at) [            ] /
dogwood       trillium       horse's tail // on Twitter Dan
Chiasson says Anne Carson affects naivety / she had
dared to write / "recently having learned to recognise
the type of tree called sycamore" / is an ecology of fresh
encounters so implausible / the house across the lake
reappears / each time the smoke clears

> *"Most of us, given a choice between chaos and*
> *naming, between catastrophe and cliché, would*
> *choose naming. Most of us see this as a zero*
> *sum game – as if there were no third place to be:*
> *something without a name is commonly thought*
> *not to exist. And here is where we can discern*
> *the benevolence of translation." – Anne Carson*

---

night translates an affect ecology

I left Srinagar on the back of a Kawasaki / Agha Shadid Ali's
family library adrift in the Jhelum / the wan of its waters
carob brown / Fatima's brother had rowed me back across
the river / apologizing for not marrying his Irish lover / "I
was too young," he said / I did not offer absolution on behalf
of another / his oars kept finding water // I wake now to the
sound of rotors / a red bucket hung from each metal midriff /
Milo staring at the hullabaloo in the sky / "I want to attend
to the world as a cat" / I write to a friend / on whose behalf
I once developed a litany of want / I knee-deep in snow / as
yoga entered his hips on a craggy hill / a blue god at his long
back / I on a sailboat / as he overlooked the Alhambra / a
Campari in his pale hand / neither of us made a good
Penelope // if ambivalence to [            ] is what it takes to
be Odysseus / we were better versed for that role / "take care
of yourself," he wrote back / in tune with the undertow //
the Kawasaki driver stopped in the valley / took photographs
of vultures diving for butcher scrap / of the soldiers who
punctuated the highway in khaki / of the stigmas of crocuses
hand-picked / "saffron tastes like the sea, beti" / an old man
whispered in my ear / when was the last time / we were
touched by its salt tongue / who do I intend to hold inside this
"we"[11] // have you ever seen Millais' *Ophelia* / palms shallow
cups of want / still willing to hold / if already given up / on
the chance to be held / there must have been a moment /
when the water kept her buoyant / the moment before / the
moment she slid

[            ]          home

                             "Could the repetition be recast?"

"It has already been established."

"How long can you go on in this vein?"

"Say again."

"Repetition operates."

"Always with the 'not.'"

"Isn't it tiring, the constant echoing?"

"Is there a number of iterations before you give up teeing?"

"Give up writing?"

"Do you think you'll die before finishing?"

"Read for repetition."

"Tweak accordingly."

"Even a magpie doesn't bring the same amethyst to the doorstep day after day."

"More Virgil, less virgules."

"The endnotes are more of the same."

"Muse, muse, muse."

"Could you follow one thread?"

"Is the persona the eye of the needle?"

"Clearly you've not read Bloom."

"What moves without the swerve?"

"Let me ask again."

"Does repetition have a colour?"

"Even the mountains repeat."

"At least hang the face on an image."

"Blue, say."

"So many stops and starts are unbecoming."

"This no reproof."

"A trail, a trial, a trail, a trial."

"You betray iteration in this manner."

it's a mistake to assign an apology / to
the category of the insincere / a friend
insists / who's to know how it inflects /
he stakes a claim in the field of his-
story / some affair / I genuflect before
my intuition / what else do I have /
"I want to say I'm sorry" / has fallen
from many lips / the intention to
express / I want to say / is not the
expression // I am sorry / I have taken
liberties with *My Life* / if there are
discrepancies always refer to the
source text / do you know me /
[whomever did not see me kiss the
mountain's foot can opt out here] // it
was not for nothing / the roads I led
you down / I wanted to feel the crud
on my palms / to host the occasional
funeral on my breath / I am / all
funeral      all breath / the sirens are
coming for me / I my own banshee //
Keats was always looking out / some
window or other / this no excuse / all
the Johns should be planting / for the
butterflies if not for the endlings /
showy milkweed / *asclepias speciosa* /
it grows taller than a short person

*"Each time
I return to the
source text,
it has changed
in my absence."*
– Lisa Robertson

---

the absence change sources always refers to the absence
change sources

I just read a poem about donkeys / "on the road to
Karpaz" / I have not mentioned my lambs / twins I bottle-
fed / until they were grown / taken to register a change
of identity / an alteration of nomenclature to make death
palatable / "pass the gravy" // over dinner Omer asks if
I am vegetarian / for the time I sat in a butcher's yard /
casualties in the rear-view mirror / clear plastic shrouds
laid out on the ground / for the time outside an abattoir /
my mind inside the serpentine // I do not ask my cabin
companion / what morning silenced his bleat / oh billy-
goat of the mantel[12] / I render as he sleeps / a curtain
drawn across / the bullseye of his body // my skirts are
infused with woodsmoke / days close with Jupiter in the
binoculars / there are flowers in the bedroom drawers /
packet after packet of seed / let the doe be sleeping / when
the bullet pierces / let her be / already horizontal / rather
than forced to fold // I work the damper back and forth /
looking for the right amount of burning / the right amount
of smoke / in another life I was the good wife / waving her
soldier off to war with good humour / a false widow left
to loiter / in long evenings' shade

The poem "about" donkeys is "How The
Dream Ends" by janan alexandra in Issue
Forty-Two of *The Adroit Journal*.

pre-light and the incantatory hum / of engines tarring /
a cracked road / I did not want to inter / an array of
feathers / or reconstitute a grave / too small for desire /
sometimes there is a road because there is an army / an
army because there are geographies // there is a cardinal
whose life lengthens in captivity[13] / the longer held the
longer its small heart / pulses inside its box of feathers /
there are many ways to be / in the confines of a body / at
lakeside the boats loll / waiting for a visitor / to remind
them of their nature // I used to think life existed in the
mind / I incline now toward hands / making them do
what the mouth proclaims / write what you love / was the
instruction given / I admit to being skeptical / not being
adept / at love      at language[14] / write as you love opens
a different dossier / every diktat with defects // as a child
my love language was watching / tadpoles in a jar /
together going nowhere on the sill / a tall ship in a corked
bottle / the latitude of every line longing / the longitude
every cross

nightfrogs eke a score out of dusk[15]

"colonoscopy drugs loosen the tongue" / Jenny tells me /
what is said when you are on the table / I am on the
table / I an amalgam of truth and infraction / I measure
my life on paper / do I write plough or plow / measure it
by the sounds the mouth lets out / bay-sil say or baz-il /
"to write is to know something," says Susan Sontag /
something can be slow to reveal itself / "Diane, the world
keeps turning" // when God had to deal with the mess of
Babel / he blamed people for their impulse to build / did
not pause to consider / the fault in his construction /
"thou madest us for Thyself," Augustine says / talking
directly to the old beard / & he was a fan / this was not
intended as critique // I looked into the bell of a temple /
that did not sound / there were words swaddled / in the
costume of my throat / at seven I was Christ's bride /
white dress    white veil    pure fiction / I have been
wrestling / with a space long dead in me / why delay the
burial / why not let the rot / don't misunderstand me /
though the veil is putaway / I am yet a sparrow / in whose
crop a prayer lives

a genealogy of the title [the newborn not licked clean of caul]:

*My Life, Delimited*

> (Replete with exemplars of the word "delimit" at work in the world. I was doing my best justification.
>
> "If possible, delimit the boundaries and let the garden bleed into its surrounding so it appears to be a seamless whole." – Tim Richardson, "Creating a 'non-garden,'" *Gardens Illustrated*
>
> "A delimiter character is usually a comma, tab, space, or semi-colon."– howtoexcel.org, *8 Ways to Split Text*
>
> "A *delimitation* addresses how a study will be narrowed in scope, that is, how it is bounded. This is the place to explain the things that you are not doing and why you have chosen not to do them …"– Frank Pajares, *The Elements of a Proposal*)

*Under a Rubric*
*My Life Delimited*

> (I cannot remember how I arrived here. Or I do not care to elucidate. One / the other.)

My Life, Delimited

Blue Flamingos

(Insert a sudden blue flamingo to
upset a monochromatic scene. A
winged cohort. A flamboyance not
yet versed in standing on a single
leg. Can you see the pose against a
sky of scattered light? I was bored
with *My Life*.)

reconceived of
multiple mouths

(Every tell blends into every other.
What is the beginning and ending
of anything? I am uninterested in
rhetorical questions at this juncture.
Tell me.)

My Life[1]

(Elizabeth Siddall was the model
for Millais' *Ophelia*. Day after day,
she sat in a tin bathtub to this end.
She almost died in the process.
To be or not to be: the endnoted
version. It is said Millais believed the
landscape to be of equal importance
to the figure. Of his thoughts on the
figure of the model, less dicta.)

My Life

(cf. I want things all the ways.)

[      ]

(An overcompensation for empty
referents. A field that extends
further than I have allowed. Think
of a figure behind glass, taking care
to balance themselves – both hands
grip the table before them. We see
the seeing seen but not the seen.
The seeing seen to be seen.)

*aboutness*

(We know the Loch Ness Monster
does not exist. Nonetheless we refer
to the fictional creature. Ergo, the
fictional Loch Ness Monster exists.
If you are so inclined, feel free to
substitute "God" for "Loch Ness
Monster" in the preceding sentences.

The home of the eponymous Nessie
has been described as *murky*. A
body of murk one part of a larger
drainage basin from where one can
gain some comprehension of
landscape formation. There are
always quantifiers lurking.)

((The question, *what is it about*,
obliges circumlocution.))

(((Can a work be announced by
a mode of articulation? Its suffix
~ness.)))

45

I thought we were done / I had wound to a close / it wouldn't be the first time[16] / I was wrong / look around / if this text were more inclined to the bold of internal titles / this page would come under the banner **Postscript** / or **I am not dead yet** // in lockdown we watched *El Barbero de Sevilla* courtesy of the Met / the location of the larynx in the throat suggests / we once used to sing / iamb      iamb      iamb // I keep trying to make / the bricolage connect / for accretion to amount to coherence / but even a narrative / & this is not that / does not accrue to a life / I understand you're tired // the attention to fragmentation can last 174 pages according to Brian Shields / this the precise length of his *Hunger Manifesto* / [I spared you] / "fail again" was the impetus I took from Beckett / still Godot did not come / "the completist is a god," says Brian Blanchfield / a beautiful phrase / committed to a relation between two false idols // I thought to retreat like a hermit crab / to hide under the stone of a certain lyric *I* / the free movement of limbs curtailed / in a manner that might amount to pleasure / we are back here again / at the hip of desire // my hypothesis is this / I will never get a measure of my hunger / there's a forever pilgrim / prostrate on my floor / the floor alternates / but the pilgrim is unmoved

> *"… and certainly the completist is a god, a just and benign one, since his plenary dominion wants nothing." – Brian Blanchfield*

the interlocutor of my psyche:

there is a problem of reference
                              Isn't there always / here. The
                              pointed to elusive / even / in
                              full view.

I mean, your choice of references, your
interlocutors – a problem, as it were, of
citation
                              Do I choose of my own accord?

                              No intervening culture?

                              I am trying to catch up with
                              *the* story.

                              *I* lead from behind.

                              Are you my interlocutor?

                              Or am I yours?

                              If a life can be written, it can
                              be rewritten.

                              This was a map and not a
                              prototype.

                              My body tells me it did not
                              begin where we are.

Has this intimacy reached?

Or does my incomplete rest.

On a wing?

Affect      on the move.

## MY BOHEMIAN IS A LEGACY
## OF DISJUNCTION

I was intent
on being
faithful

to every bone rattle
every cradle country
every dead-end

but roads give back
what grief they are given
threefold

levy time's toll

I could end
every poem
"and yet"

and yet
my longshore self

still stands
at a wharf

watching
infolding

I learnt my lexicon
by a lighthouse.

Many mouths
flowed
into
one mouth:

a black box,
a jumble
of echoes.

~

Jays mimic
the osprey. The musicians
sleep late.

They don't wake
in a context
of suspicion.

~

Borborygmus
in the belly.

Jonah, fall back
now. Time

to please
another vernacular,

a voice-over
substructure.

In the beginning
you give away
the only world
you know. Night
inside a belly. Full
picture, surround
sound. In the beginning,
birth gives birth
to an amniotic
historian. The night
is a memory you cannot
language. It wants
a construction you
cannot limn. In the
beginning, grief flows in
to the freehold
of your bone.
All your life
you look for a vessel
to in turn
hold you – the soft spots
return. In the beginning,
the ending is
a given. A platter
to a late room. A coda
on a silent
piano. A nocturnal
dumb-show.

I

How same each night unfolds. I wake in a cavity of darkness.
My bag of blood and bone in a twist. A house of plastic
subject to wind's dictation. Horses on retinal backs. Flyspecks
on flanks. No intention to be on history's tail. Once upon a
time I slept like a foal. My cradle of grasses rocked by breezes.
Waking in tears at intervals. Fluid on my fat cheeks. Hunger
saddled to gut. Before words found a path to the mouth.

2

Snow clouds slink across the lake. Disappear what orientates.
In summer it was by way of smoke. The last word of pine
calligraphed in the sky. Weather is never neutral. Tell my
body this is not personal. My senses fold under the bough.
In this crouch a quietus of sound. Last winter, or was it the
one before, I opened a man's duffel. Snuck my hands around
his wasted centre. This how we coded goodbye. Temperature
slides. Below freezing regardless of how you language snow.
Prism. Dendrite. Flake. Fall.

3

I was born on May Day. Snow fell from the sky. On an
island of coastlines that lacked an intimacy with translucent
weather. Snow now half my calendar. The benign glades of
the page. Tonight's lullaby a distant sea. Several mountain
passes negotiate the difference. To skies that open. To waves
that call and respond. Murmurrings under a coverlet of brine.
Home, what is it. Salt is good for a cut. Lower-case mercy
to soften a forfeit.

4

I line my mouth with words. Brittle plasters for what nights
bite open. Reptilian brain awake inside the horizontal. Early
patterns built into sleep's cracks. Landscape bleached of
colour. What sort of *I* lives here? In this outhouse. Next to
the dormant skunkweed. Designs locked in time's weave.
Vials of sand passed from dream hand to dream hand.
Mandrem. Howth. Red Sands.


5

The toilet of another shipping container flushes its sound
to my bed. On my first day in La Paz, a woman squawked
in my face. Slit my bag with a blade. The weight of water
inside gave her away. Caul is the sound of experience I am
after. On the trail of. Another geography promised another
self. Or it promised nothing and I was the Queen of Swords.
One hand beckoning butterflies; one hand sword and stern.
Portraiture a loose knot. I not tight. Nor undone.


6

Where do you place your commas? In the deep of your
nervous system. In your three-pound brain. The desire is
to get out of the drain. I used to kneel in a wooden pew.
My gaze stuck on the altar. Now I riffle through old
photographs on repeat. The world in sepia makes sense
to me. Do you believe in prayer? The memory of hunger
is a body. Mayday. Mayday.

1

In the yard a green pump. I lift the handle to siphon memory.
Diary trips to the dairy. Mother sold eggs to the neighbours.
How much a dozen? What is the cost of connection? Fifty-
four bones are not enough to hold time.

2

The cat of the car-house had perceptual sleep in her eyes.
One day she was gone. We didn't talk about what was
known in bone. God's resignation tendered prematurely.
It took time for sinew. To catch up. Catch on.

3

From the intercom in the kitchen, you could eavesdrop on
parturition. Gradients of wail to hail degrees of arrival. Only
once did I smack a calf into being. Pulled back the turmeric
amnion to let the eyes. Lid to light.

4

Certain nights men with lamps paced the fields as in an
underworld simulation. I do not call myself exile. I work to
break the nocturnal animal. To entangle time with a snare.
No small game.

5

I repeat the rain which repeats. Its beat on galvanise. Did I
ever step into the heart of a puddle? My niece in her unicorn
boots fathoms joy. We scoff berries from the ditch on the way
home from school. Hers, mine; hers, mine.

## 6

An aerial photograph of the house hung on the living room
wall. History in black and white. An alternate cosmology
beyond the frame. A concrete patch lamp-lit for the chicks.
A large sun to their Lilliputian size.

## 7

The poet wrote the nation into being was the politic I was
sold. Yeats, another God the father. Emer jealous of the sea
goddess. Blah, blah, blah. I learnt this one detail later.
Historiography a preference. A bent.

## 8

The bull in the field of memory stands still. There is a
chronology I know and a chronology I am. Cemeteries
bloom. Bluebells, roses, daffodils. The slip of matter. From
one locale to another. The new configuration.

On this vessel of refuge
I lay down. Blessed be

he who delivers me
in the garden

my whole-flesh
corruption.

~

How long shall I sleep
the sleep of rejoice?

I am
shaken.

~

Answer desire.
Name your petition.

~

I am fret and stir
all day long.

Mouth, solve my ransom
life. Make me

a nothing shadow
fool for you.

~

At the sound
of thunder,

take cover. Bird
among the branches.

The moon sets the forest
to its labour. A form

to play in. A fetter
of rule and bind.

~

The daughters of judgment
are high. Gift them

a melody to answer
the statute. Who dares

to mother a strange
language? To push against

the gated register.

~

Do not court silence.
Attack my prayer.

Does an accuser not count
as sin plunder? I am

locust. My body
devours the ground.

~

I long in wild places,
double-bind flesh

to unfold. I stream
and small, cry and cute.

I am any kind of fool
for creation.

~

Do I sheep
your tongue?

I pray like a fowler
filled with laughter.

First the quiver,
then the shot.

~

I trouble
and persevere.

I am blood, venom,
plot. I eat

these delicacies. Death
long enough.

The collision of mucous membranes, he said. An incidence
of touch so maligned. Should I not feel pleasure again?
The hummingbird falls over and over for the bee balm. For the
colour of expansion. The universe is slipping – away from us.
Do wolves howl more at a full moon? Or is it I am primed to
hear them? At the neighbour's stable, a mesh hangs from the
beam like macramé. Three heads stuffed in its weave. An
always ache for the coffer. Muzzle to muzzle, mare and
stallion barter. If it's not one hunger, it's another. I like a
tongue all up in my mouth. If you want to argue wolves,
the dark will be spent in dispute. I have violet notions.
To rend the monochrome. To aberrate.

what is the funding of this diction
the hidden coinage

this parachute is my determinant
    [please another verge]

I dabble in fairytale accounting
       ["Alack, what poverty my Muse brings forth ..."]

*la-da-dee*

I might feel more homeowner
if I could learn
the irrelevance of cud

    *la-dah-dah*

"chew      on dirt
the forest floor is sweet"

an invitation to taste
soil content

not meant to agitate
a constitution

One day love brings a quart of cherries
from the Okanagan in a saddlebag,

ruby suns swaddled in reams of brown paper
to keep the tender from bruising,

the next there's only pit
and the biodegradable clamshell

topping the compost rot
like a crown.

There is a story in Irish myth about how a warrior woos Emer.
The warrior-hero attacks the fort of Emer's father in order
   to *get the girl*.
Emer's father leaps off a wall in an effort to escape.
He is successful in this endeavour in so far as death is a kind
   of escape.
Everybody is happy in this rendition because love.
Later the prize will be a fertile brown bull.
For now it is the girl.
The girl's fertility is not stated explicitly.

_____ (**Your name**)

Choose one from the following options:
   a) All life is valuable and should not be slaughtered –
      this includes the bull.
   b) The life that gives life is the most valuable.
   c) Schopenhauer was a great writer who pushed an
      old woman down the stairs (her noise interrupted
      his writing life).
   d) The function of fertility is to express the life.

Choose one from the following options:
   a) I could define "copacetic" if my life depended on it.
   b) My life depends on it.
   c) "Rendition" was my clue that not everything
      was copacetic.
   d) What?

## II INFLECTION

(after *Lovers*, 1984–92 by Howard Hodgkin)


(i)

it takes years
to settle
on a palette

& this
before the subject
enters

but chronology
bores
the lover

(ii)

flex of wrist
folds compliments

one into the concave
of the other

(iii)

the mantle
pulled back

      in quiet hands

to limn the geography
beneath

(iv)

this copse
of green grasses

this morning
       & this mountain

this skein
of this skin

(v)

who does this bid
you remember?

this slip
       & this elision

(vi)

"the painting is finished
when the subject returns"

(vii)

in the rear-view

       telegraph poles
       blur

into vapour

I find Vermeer on the coffee table     *Woman in Blue Reading
a Letter*     brass bullet points on Spanish chairs     the artist
partial to an accent in a room     a standing order in a broader
furniture     a signpost     a return     why I loiter in this
parallel womb     rocking rocking     above the mantel a
billy goat     stares out the skylight     like an outcast who
sees in every bluff     an armature to hang a life on     there
are so many rags stuffed in my hide     a horde of dead sailors
in my hull     bluejackets     yellow jackets     stung princes
in ramshackle cabins     I try to weather     the bow of
constant quarrels     in the crosswinds of my mind     *is trestle
related to trust*     Thomas asks on the old rail trail     trestle
from Old French *trestle*     meaning crossbeam     where a
material spans an opening     a relation can be conceived
this is a practical birthing     against the grain of etymology
I kneel to sniff the creosote     like every dumb animal
chasing a scent or a vision     what was Beethoven thinking
or did he move from question     *muss es sein?*     to assertion
*es muss sein!*     to sound out spirit     I can hear the flicker
pick ants from the telegraph pole     repetition no cure for
hunger     my foil will return     shake again his head     at
the pots on the deck     *basil, such a princess*     a lexical sting
in the nest     how I want him all the same     the spicy globe
and summerlong     hot on the fall tongue

This fledgling state, this ongoing metamorphosis –
nobody said becoming was quick.

> You ask if I fly in my sleep, forget all grounding
> by way of dream.

This has been no easy consecration:

rites may need
revisiting

in the wake of flukes that breach,

bellows that resurrect
wingspan.

> You ask what's the hurry, look to exposed brick,
> run your hand the length of its filament.

How can I argue
with touch so deliberate?

And yet. And yet.

1

morning broken open by chainsaw / I handpick twigs / from
this curated nest / you can be born again / if not from the
womb / from the wound / if not from the wound / from its
echo / in every wager and every water / an elongated winter
in the wake / ossification complete / memory jammed in
sutures / how fall reverberates / the fell renegotiating space

2

swifts descend on the evening chimney / scissor the air clear /
a collocation of confinement / in the soot throat / Beckett
understood / the nothingness that leans / fast into ruin / the
mind that spills

3

you think too much said a friend / an assertion she has long
forgotten / knowing nothing of how words cure / I cannot
forget / I was born of a breach / into the wound of a body /
I wish and wallow in this immurement / thrash against its
frame / only a tiny stone to orient / listen otolith / the body
is an anchorite / solitary in space

4

ravens at the outflow / caw for the channel / to spit the
redfish out / the beach a potter's field / gills stained in
hoarfrost / sockets picked clean / further along the strand /
a child takes a line for a walk / drags a stick through sand

5

the naturalist names / the birds we hear / nuthatch chickadee
oh a wren / an excerpt from the aviary of her brain / the
dipper's head goes under / the ribbon of water / does
the animal smell the relict / or listen past / the decibels of
water / to the pitch beyond rot

6

the chickadees emerge / from the charred birch / careen close
to the scalp / a caress to raise a coffin lid / blue moves around
the body / like water like grief / the sunflowers fall over / the
long of their own stems                    .

7

the girl holds a conch shell / to the mallet of her ear / even the
gift of the sea / is received as salt / cruelty a child not told /
the one hundred iterations of placenta / the one hundred and
eight beads of mala / ricochet off the ground / each rose
quartz tear-drop an anemone / a daughter of the wind

8

a northern pygmy scans the skyline / for satiety in the form
of a songbird / it's not yet nightfall / not yet winter /
Persephone packs her bags for the underground / does she
love / what she walks toward / how long does it take / to
acclimate to darkness's depth / where the eternal unseen /
doula of breach / awaits his ward of division

9

maples set against snow clouds / the leaves golden / the cold
ancient / I wrote love in Ogham / painted shaky lines with my
unlovely hands / waves across a spine / the vortex of emptiness
swells / the last leaves resist separation / cleave to the bough

10

the golf course follows / the topography of ground / the pond
an imperfect oval / edged with reeds / the tallest sisters fold
over the scab / no wildflowers in attendance / no songbirds
at the ear / oh for a sister / to split loyalty beyond water /
crimson laughter lines bleed / from the woodpecker's beak

11

icicles grip a fallen log / a season hard with knowing / my
love conceived / in a dusk of brine / mimics the mute snow /
only the brass fish hazards to intervene / plinks against the
post / when the wind lifts / its small frame

12

mountains stretch / on all sides / the sky a sieve / all day
long / no poem ever ends Valéry says / the tide comes in
comes in comes in / this long-drawn christening

dusk is full
of animal,

the bloodrush
warmth,

a language
in the nightthroat.

we climb
the roughwood,

peel bark
with the disks
of our feet,

listen
on waking

for rain
on the canopy.

Night-blooming jasmine
assails the proboscis

of the late walker.
Where are you taking me

lampless satellite?
My lists asleep,

our odyssey
in the frame.

You needle
as I listen

for echoes
like a bat.

I didn't want
to come here.

I thought
we were finished
with this.

# ACKNOWLEDGMENTS

The Elizabeth Bishop poem referenced on page 22 is from "Questions of Travel" in which she writes, "Should we have stayed at home and thought of here?" (*Questions of Travel*, FSG, 1965).

"the completist is a god" is from Brian Blanchfield's "On Completism" (*Proxies: Essays Near Knowing*, Nightboat, 2016).

The Anne Carson quote on page 34 is from the essay "Variations on the Right to Remain Silent" (*Nay Rather*, Sylph Editions, 2013). "Recently having learned to recognise the type of tree called sycamore" is from her poem "Life" (*New Yorker*, June 2021).

"What is the mind of the Greeks and you concerning my life" is from Euripides' *Trojan Women*, translated by M. Hadas and J. McLean (Bantam Books, 1965).

The Luce Irigaray quote is from "This sex which is not one," translated by Claudia Reeder, in *New French Feminisms*, edited by Elaine Marks and Isabelle de Courtivron (University of Massachusetts Press, 1980).

The Lisa Robertson quote is from *Anemones: A Simone Weil Project* (If I Can't Dance, I Don't Want To Be Part Of Your Revolution, 2021).

"Alack, what poverty my Muse brings forth" is from
Sonnet 103 by William Shakespeare.

"If it be rags, let it be rags" is from "Don't Wed"
by Taras Shevchenko, translated by John Weir.

"To write is to know something" is from "At the Same
Time: The Novelist and Moral Reasoning" from Susan
Sontag's *At The Same Time: Essays and Speeches*
(FSG, 2007).

The Jun'ichirō Tanizaki quotes are from *In Praise of
Shadows*, translated by Thomas Harper (Leete's Island
Books, 1977).

"no nation now but the imagination" is from Derek
Walcott's "The Schooner Flight" (*Selected Poems,* FSG,
2007), while "every I is a fiction finally" comes from
*Omeros* (FSG, 1990).

Thanks to the Writers' Trust of Canada who published
a section of this work under the title "*My Life,
Delimited.*" Other selections were previously published
in *Marble Poetry Magazine* ("inflection"), *Skylight 47*
("tree frogs"), *wildness* ("This (Dream of) Flying"),
*Lammergeier*, and *The Ex-Puritan*. With gratitude to
the editors of these publications.

Thanks to Denver Jermyn and Merry Benezra for their
insights and for the timely reminder that reading is writing.

Thanks Radha Neilson for sharing her attention
to airborne creatures.

Thanks to editor Carolyn Smart for assistance in bringing *aboutness* to something approaching stasis.

Thanks Tara Cunningham for circling the drain of religion, poesis, and miscellany with me not infrequently – a "not" for the road.